Jim & Shorty

Jim & Shorty

Alex Pock-Goldin

Jim and Shorty
first published 2008 by
Scirocco Drama
An imprint of J. Gordon Shillingford Publishing Inc.

Scirocco Drama Editor: Glenda MacFarlane
Cover design by Terry Gallagher / Doowah Design Inc.
Cover photo by John Paskievich (originally published in *The North End*, University of Manitoba Press, 2007)
Author photo by Tim Leyes
Production photos by Massimo Pannarale
Printed and bound in Canada on 100% post-consumer recycled paper.

We acknowledge the financial support of the Manitoba Arts Council, The Canada Council for the Arts and the Government of Canada through the Book Publishing Industry Development Program (BPIDP) for our publishing program.

Production inquiries should be addressed to:
Production inquiries should be addressed to:
Michael Petrasek
Kensington Literary Representation
34 Andrew Street
Toronto, ON M5T 1K6
(416) 979-0187
kensingtonlit@rogers.com

Library and Archives Canada Cataloguing in Publication

Poch-Goldin, Alex
Jim and Shorty / Alex Poch-Goldin.

A play.
ISBN 978-1-897289-31-0

I. Title.

PS8581.O15J54 2008 C812'.6 C2008-903562-3

J. Gordon Shillingford Publishing
P.O. Box 86, RPO Corydon Avenue, Winnipeg, MB Canada R3M 3S3

For Chloe Babette

Alex Poch-Goldin

Alex is an award-winning playwright and actor. His plays include *Yahrzeit* (*Jahrestag*) which won the 2003 Toronto Jewish Playwriting Award. The play completed a 2008 national tour of Germany. His play *Cringeworthy* was nominayed for five Dora Awards including Outstanding New Play. His other plays include *Anybody and Nobody*, *Going* (with Kelly Thornton) and *This Hotel,* produced at Theatre Passe Muraille and nominated for six Dora Awards including Outstanding New Play. *Jim and Shorty* was adapted by him and filmed for Bravo! Television in 2001. Alex was commissioned by the CBC to write an original radio drama, *The Death of Simon Pinchuk,* which was recorded and broadcast nationally in 2005. He has written his first feature film script, *Jacob's Dream,* and two libretti: *Lisa,* produced at the 2002 Opera America Conference, and *The Shadow,* slated for production in 2009. He is currently developing his new play *The Right Road to Pontypool*. Alex is also an acclaimed actor and trained in Montreal at The Dome Theatre/Dawson College. He has worked extensively in film, television, radio and on stages across Canada. He lives and works in Toronto with his partner Kelly Thornton and their scrumptious daughter Chloe Babette.

Characters

Jim

Shorty (also known as Macy)

Big Tom—an Aboriginal Canadian

Setting

Act 1: A park bench in autumn

Act 2: A park bench in winter

Production Information

Jim and Shorty premiered at The Factory Studio Theatre in Toronto on February 3, 2000. It was a Planet 88 Production in association with Factory Theatre and had the following cast:

SHORTY.. Earl Pastko
JIM .... Ron Gabriel
BIG TOM... Lorne Cardinal

Directed by Layne Coleman
Set and Costumes Design by Sherri Hay
Lighting Design by Steve Lucas
Stage Management by Kristin McCollum
Produced by Kelly Thornton

Jim and Shorty premiered in its one act format at the 1998 Summerworks Festival in Toronto with the same cast. The production was directed by Alex Poch-Goldin. The play was then filmed for Spoken Art and aired on Bravo! Television.

Special Thanks

Kelly Thornton, Ken Gass, David Baile, Factory Theatre, Layne Coleman, Earl Pastko, Ron Gabriel, Lorne Cardinal, Sarah Stanley, Ed Roy, Gary Farmer, Buddies in Bad Times, Theatre Passe Muraille, The Canada Council for the Arts and anyone who helped in any way.

Prologue

Lights come up on TOM. He addresses the audience.

TOM: You find his name and you make an X. Then you drop it in the box. And they'll count 'em up—and the more that does it the better. They'll count 'em up and if he wins. Boy, it'll be somethin'. They'll all come downtown, from all over and build a big fire. Throw in bottles and tires, take off their clothes and throw them in too. They'll dance naked and burn sweetgrass. Hunh. Sing songs. Then they'll sit in a big circle and pass the pipe. And it'll get passed to everyone, everyone'll smoke. And when mornin' comes, that's when he'll show. He'll take off his shoes and step into the circle, his eyes glowin' with all his people around him. He'll unbend his spirit, raise up his hands and say somethin' like "Brothers and sisters. It is a new day. A day of change. A day to be awake." *(Beat.)* Find his name and make an X.

Black out.

Act I

Scene 1

Lights come up on MACY sitting on the bench rubbing his leg. Autumn leaves are scattered on the ground. He begins to roll a cigarette removing tobacco and papers from his sock. JIM approaches counting change. They are both shabbily dressed. MACY wears an old suit, the pants have no pockets, Jim has unmatched pants, a jacket and a tight T-shirt. JIM looks out in the distance. He eventually turns to MACY.

JIM: 'Member the beer store used to be there? *(Pause.)* It's gone now. *(Pause.)* Used ta be able to buy all kinds 'a beer there. Cold. *(Pause.)* Those were the good old days. *(Pause.)* No more pints. No big bottles. Now it's all little bottles, you drink a little, you say, Where'd it all go?

MACY: Yah. *(Pause.)*

JIM: Not like the old days. Everythin' wasn't nearly as expensive as now. Those were times. *(Pause.)* I remember buyin' beer at that store. Cold.

MACY: Colder 'n hell.

JIM: Oh jeez, yah. Not in cans like today. Those were good days.

MACY: Oh yah. That store's all different now.

JIM: What is it a gas station?

MACY: Donut Shop. World King Donuts.

JIM: Jeez. My girlfriend makes E-clairs, so good. You take one bite, all your teeth fall out.

(Pause.) Donuts and beer is good. Donuts and beer and a coffee. Donuts and a cigarette. You like donuts?

MACY: I like food of any kind.

JIM: Gotta smoke?

MACY: Las' one.

JIM: I like a cigarette with dessert. *(Pause.)* Watchin' the TV. *(Pause.)*

That wrestlin's not as good before, too many commercials. *(Pause.)* How're you smokin' that thing?

MACY: There's no one way ta smoke.

JIM: Gimme a cigarette.

MACY: I got no more.

JIM: Smoke it slow. Slower. You gotta make it last. Nice slow smoke. You got nowheres to go, you gotta make it last. *(He takes the cigarette.)* See look.

MACY: Gimme that.

JIM: I'm just showin' ya is all.

MACY: Showin' me how to lose my cigarette.

Pause.

JIM: Got any pennies?

MACY: No.

Pause.

JIM: You goin' to the tavern tonight?

MACY shrugs.

Well you try'n get there. Got specials tonight.

MACY: Oh jeez what's today?

JIM: Don't know.

MACY: I got a meeting.

JIM: Who ya meeting?

MACY: Worker.

JIM: Oh yah. What's your number?

MACY: Forty four. What's yours?

JIM: Zero. Know where the office is now?

MACY: Two blocks.

JIM: No, closed that one.

MACY: Closed what?

JIM: The welfare.

MACY: When?

JIM: Las' month. Got a brand new buildin' they put up. All central now. Everyone's goes to the same place. My girl frien' goes.

MACY: Never.

JIM: Oh yah. All downtown now. Used to have 'em everywhere. *(Pause.)* Nice lookin buildin'.

MACY: When d'it change?

JIM: Gotta smoke?

MACY: Las' one.

JIM: Gimme puff.

MACY: Hang on.

JIM: Yer name's Shorty right.

MACY: No.

JIM: I thought yer name was Shorty.

MACY: No. Macy.

JIM: Oh.

MACY: My middle name's Shorty.

JIM: Oh. That's it. *(Pause.)* I'm trying to save enough to buy some beer. How much is a beer?

MACY: About a dollar.

JIM: Jeez a dollar a beer! Never thought I'd live to see it. How much is twenty-four?

MACY: I don't know. How much ya got?

JIM: Seventy eight cents.

MACY: Keep savin'. *(Pause.)*

JIM: You gettin' a cheque today?

MACY: Two o'clock.

JIM: You better get goin'.

MACY: What time is it?

JIM: Don't know. Must be gettin' on.

MACY: After this smoke.

JIM: How're you getting downtown?

MACY: Bus.

JIM: You got money?

MACY: Ticket.

JIM: Where'd you get it?.

MACY: Found it.

JIM: Geez lucky guy. Some things never change.

MACY: You gettin' a cheque?

JIM: Got kicked off.

MACY: How come?

JIM: Missed an appointment.

MACY: Oh yah. Where ya staying?

JIM: Sister's. With her husband.

MACY: Where's that?

JIM: Over there.

MACY: Oh yah. She married?

JIM: Who?

MACY: Yer sister.

JIM: Yah.

MACY: Pretty?

JIM: Nah.

MACY: I gotta sister.

JIM: Pretty?

MACY: Jeez yah. Saw her couple'a years back.

JIM: Married?

MACY: Don't know.

JIM: Mine's is stupid and married.

MACY: Mine's pretty though.

JIM: Born that way. Stupid.

MACY: Why's she stupid?

JIM: *(Beat.)* I gotta girl. She's gettin' a cheque.

MACY: Pretty?

JIM: Nah.

Pause.

MACY: When'd that beer store close?

JIM: Don't know. It's all central now. Everyone's goes to the same place. Near the welfare. Used to be able to buy beer all over, now one place.

MACY: It's changed eh?

JIM: Jeez yah. *(Pause.)* You gonna vote?

MACY: What for?

JIM: Yah.

MACY: What's the election?

JIM: New guy.

MACY: They're all the same eh? I'm telling ya.

JIM: Jeez, don't tell me.

(Pause.) Heard an Indian's running.

Pause.

MACY: Did ya try to get back on?

JIM: What?

MACY: The system.

JIM: Oh yah. My worker… What's your number?

(l to r): Ron Gabriel (Jim) and Earl Pastko (Shorty)

MACY: Forty four.

JIM: Yah not her, another one. She sent me to a doctor. You know. For my head. All kinds of questions. Personal, you know. Finally she says "All's you care about is gettin' drunk". I said "Ain't that why I'm here? "Now I gotta wait for a disabled benefits. Eight week penalty for being disable. Jeez hit me with a stick why don'tcha.

MACY: Still gotta wait eight weeks.

JIM: Only three left. That's why I'm at my sister's. I sure could eat.

MACY: Got a Chinese and Indian across from the club.

JIM: What club?

MACY: Where I'm stayin'.

JIM: Ain't ya got a place? Lucky guy like you.

MACY: Sure the club. Cheap. Don't get half as much stolen.

JIM: Is Rich at the club still?

MACY: Rich? Rich who?

JIM: Tall fella, silver hair. Goes by the name of Rich.

MACY: Don't know him.

JIM: Silver hair. Tall. He's always smilin' and janglin' pennies.

MACY: Jeez no, he died.

JIM: Died eh? Jeez. His liver?

MACY: Don't know. But he's all dead now. Died a few months back.

JIM: Thought I saw him last week.

MACY: Was he dead?

JIM: No.

MACY: Then you ain't seen him.

(Pause.) He's in a better place now.

JIM: Where?

MACY: Sittin' up with the angels.

JIM: Angels eh?

MACY: All the food he can eat. Lots 'a beer and blankets.

JIM: Smokes?

MACY: Sure. That's what clouds is. Angels smokin'.

MACY begins to roll a final cigarette.

JIM: Hunh. Don't say. See that one. 'Prob'ly my old man. He liked ta smoke. Smoked 'til his lung caved in. Died with a cigarette in his mouth. When they found him his lips was burned.

MACY: Aw jeez.

JIM: Yah. He liked to smoke. Three packs a day. Back when they was cheap. Nowdays ya gotta mortgage just'a buy a pack.

MACY: That's why I roll 'em. Healthier too.

JIM: Don't say. Roll me one.

MACY: When I get my cheque I'll give ya a smoke.

JIM: These packs ya see in the garbage. Beware of smoking. Smoking causes something. Smoking can harm your sister's baby.

MACY: My ma smoked pregnant.

JIM: Mine's did too. Didn't do me no harm.

(Short pause.) Soon you'll gotta go downtown just to buy 'em.

MACY: You ain't kidding.

JIM: I ain't kidding.

MACY: What's yer name?

JIM: Jim.

MACY: That's a good name. Always liked that name. Short.

JIM: To the point. Jim.

MACY: What're your friends call you.

JIM: Jim.

MACY: Mine's call me Shorty.

JIM: I thought that was your name. I seen ya at the tavern ain't I?

MACY: Which one?

JIM: Over there.

MACY: Oh yah I been there.

JIM: You goin' tonight?

MACY: I don't know. *(Pause.)*

JIM: Wanna come over to my sister's?

MACY: Nah.

JIM: I'll get her to cook. She stupid but she cooks.

MACY: What's she make?

JIM: She makes a good chicken pie. Creamy.

MACY: No.

JIM: Yah.

MACY: Haven't had chicken pie in a long time. It's all chemical now.

JIM: Not my stupid sister's. She buys the crust 'n fills it up with chicken. Right to the top.

MACY: Chicken.

JIM: Mmmm.

MACY: I like chicken.

JIM: Couple 'a beers, some chicken pie. That's livin'. *(Beat.)* So Rich is dead eh?

MACY: That's what I hear. Still an empty cot at the club.

JIM: I gotta bed at my sister's. But she went to vote so's I had to get outta the house.

MACY: How come?

JIM: I needed a walk anyway. *(Pause.)*

MACY: Got the time?

JIM: Oh sure. *(Pause.)*

MACY: Gotta head downtown.

JIM: It's early yet, where ya running. Sit a bit.

MACY: All right. Then I gotta go.

JIM: Me too. That pie'll be bakin' up some soon. *(Pause.)*

MACY: Where'd ya get the money?

JIM: Workin'. I got a quarter from a phone. I found a dime on the sidewalk. That's…how much is that?

MACY: A dime and a quarter makes thirty five.

JIM: My sister gimme a quarter. That's what?

MACY: A quarter and a quarter is fifty and a dime?

JIM: Found a dime.

MACY: Is sixty.

JIM: Yah. Then I made fifteen playing harmonica is?

MACY: Fifteen and sixty is…seventy five.

JIM: And that's how much I got.

MACY: Gotta save money ta make money.

JIM: Gotta save money to buy beer. If I had a lotta money I'd buy a lotta beer. And a boat. And sunglasses.

MACY: Nothing worth buyin'. Had this suit eight years. How many suits a fellow needs?

JIM: Only one.

MACY: That's right. Can only wear one at a time. College graduate at the welfare. Makin' thirty thousand a year. Sittin' wearin' a T-shirt last time I was in. A government employee. Time's sure change. No tie neither.

JIM: Jeez. The government eh?

MACY: That's why I don't vote.

JIM: You know that Indian?

MACY: Which Indian?

JIM: Tom.

MACY: Tom?

JIM: Big Tom. Tom Tom. Big Indian.

MACY: No.

JIM: Big Indian. Tall. He's at the tavern all'a time.

MACY: No.

JIM: Jeez you know him Shorty. Big tall Indian. At the tavern.

MACY: *(Beat.)* Oh yah.

JIM: He's the one told me 'bout the election. He went ta vote. He says to me "Jim, take it from a native." That's what they're called now, not Indians no more, "Jim, the only way you'se can change things is by voting. You don't vote, nothin' changes. Indians ain't got nothin' for everythin' they gave up except now we can vote. And today we're gonna vote in an Indian and things are gonna change!"

MACY: Nobody's gonna elect no Indian in the government.

JIM: Well don't tell Tom that. He'll crack you over the head. He's big. *(Beat.)* My family been in this country two hundred years. Came over on a boat, ya know. And there was plenty of Indians around then. Don't see so many now.

MACY: They're at the club.

JIM: Yah?

MACY: Sure lots of 'em.

JIM: What do they do?

MACY: Sit around. *(Pause.)* You gonna vote?

JIM: Maybe. *(Pause.)*

MACY: You gotta card?

JIM: Sure, them finger prints cards. That's all you need. It's all computers now. It's all hooked up.

MACY: All's someone's gotta do is push a button and it's all gone.

JIM: Naw, they got it all backed up now. You can't fool the government. They're backed up.

MACY: Gotta friend collects two cheques.

JIM: Two? Lucky guy.

MACY: Government don't know. Pretended he only had one arm, so they fingerprinted his left hand. He's clearing eight hundred a month.

JIM: Jeez. He going to the tavern tonight?

MACY: Prob'ly.

JIM: I'd like to meet him. *(Pause.)* Can you buy one beer at a time?

MACY: No. It's like smokes. You gotta buy twenty-four at a time.

JIM: Why's that?

MACY: It's trade.

JIM: Trade eh? What do you get for voting?

MACY: Nothin'.

JIM: Nothin'? Then what's the point?

MACY: There ain't no point. That's why I don't vote.

JIM: If people got somethin' you'd think more people'd vote.

MACY: Sure. That's trade.

Pause.

JIM: You can smell them donuts. Fresh.

MACY: Sure smells good.

JIM: How much is a donut?

MACY: Don't know. About a dollar.

JIM: A dollar! Jeez. A dollar. You could have a beer for a dollar, why'd ya want a donut?

MACY: Gotta eat.

JIM: Yah.

MACY: Gotta have a balance. Yer venchtables. Yer protein. Yer liquids. Yer…

JIM: Is donuts a protein?

MACY: No donuts is. I don't know what they is. They fry it in venchtable oil so maybe it's a venchtable.

JIM: A dollar for a venchtable! Least ya only gotta buy one.

MACY: Yah, but ya buy twelve they give ya thirteen.

JIM: Why they do that?

MACY: Baker's dozen. Ya buy twelve they give ya thirteen.

Pause.

JIM: Wish they did that with beer. You sure yer gettin' a cheque?

MACY: Sure. I'm getting a cheque.

JIM: Hope yer right. Marge got kicked off.

MACY: Who's Marge.

JIM: My girl.

MACY: Ain't yer girl gettin' a cheque?

JIM: Ya now, but she got kicked off.

MACY: How'd she get back on?

JIM: She had to go to a lot of meetings.

MACY: Jeez I hate that.

JIM: Yah.

MACY: She pretty?

JIM: Nah.

MACY: Where'd ya meet her?

JIM: At the bar.

MACY: Oh yah.

JIM: *(Pause.)* 'Member that night when that guy had the fit?

MACY: No.

JIM: You was there. Guy fell over, hit the table. Beer spilled all over. Had an epilectric fit. Cops came 'n took him away.

MACY: *(Beat.)* Oh yah.

JIM: That's when I met Marge. *(Pause.)* She used ta be with him.

MACY: Hunh. I better get going soon.

JIM: What time is it?

MACY: I don't know.

JIM: How ya goin'?

MACY: Bus.

JIM: Which one?

MACY: The one goes right downtown.

JIM: How much is a bus now?

MACY: Three dollars.

JIM: Three dollars! Jeez. You could eat and have two beers just fer gettin' on a bus. Or three beers.

MACY: Can't even buy tickets at the store now. Gotta go to them ticket places.

JIM: How much is a ticket?

MACY: Three dollars.

JIM: Jeez. Might as well not buy a ticket if it costs the same.

MACY: Need a ticket.

JIM: What for?

MACY: To get on the bus. Gotta have a ticket. It's trade.

JIM: *(Beat.)* I don't need a ticket. I ain't goin' nowhere.

(Pause.) My stupid sister's husban' drives a bus.

MACY: That's a good job.

JIM: Yah but he's stupid. I tell ya Shorty. I get on the bus once. He's drivin'. I say "Hey give your old brother in law a ride". He says "If ya ain't got a ticket ya ain't gettin' a ride". My own brother in law.

MACY: I know a bus driver. Who's yer brother in law?

JIM: My sisters husban'.

MACY: No. What's his name?

JIM: I don't know. Stupid. His name's stupid.

MACY: My old man worked for the city.

JIM: What'd he do?

MACY: Collected garbage.

JIM: That's a good job.

MACY: Used ta find lots a stuff. Good stuff. People throw out lots a good stuff. Had a whole house full of people's garbage. All good.

(l to r): Earl Pastko (Shorty) and Ron Gabriel (Jim)

JIM: Jeez that's a good job. I gotta get my own place. I'm sick of my sister's stupid apartment. Once I'm officially disabled I'm moving out.

MACY: Get one 'a those motor carts.

JIM: What carts?

MACY: Th'lectric ones. You see 'em outside the tavern. Like a motor cycle.

JIM: Oh yah I seen 'em.

MACY: You can drive anywhere. Downtown, the park. Carry beer in it.

JIM: Yah that'd be good. I'm tired of walkin'. Look at my shoes. They just hang.

MACY: Good shoes is a priority. Get yer girl to buy ya some.

JIM: Marge? Never met a cheaper girl. Stingey. When I got money don't I spread it around, buy everyone drinks?

MACY: I don't know.

JIM: Well I do. Plenty times. When ya don't got money everybody forgets about you!

MACY: It's a personal thing.

JIM: Your whole life goes and what do ya got?

MACY: Ya ain't sick.

JIM: No I ain't sick.

MACY: That's somethin'.

JIM: Who said I was sick?

MACY: Nobody.

JIM: Right nobody. I ain't sick. Anyone says I is, is a liar.

MACY: Ya got a place to stay.

JIM: Yah my sister.

MACY: That's something.

JIM: *(Beat.)* Sure is.

Pause.

MACY: Well, I gotta go.

JIM: Where to?

MACY: The welfare.

JIM: Oh yah. How long'll you be?

MACY: Don't know. Depends on the line.

JIM: Jeez I hate them lines. Don't they put it right in the bank now?

MACY: If ya got a bank. Went ta open one and they told me I needed a credit card?

JIM: What for.

MACY: To get an account.

JIM: If ya got a credit card why'd ya need welfare?

MACY: Exactly. An' I got the finger print card and all. I wouldn't have a credit card if I had a thousand dollars.

JIM: How come?

MACY: It's all owing. In a trade situation you give them your money you take your thing. With a card you take your thing but you still owe the money.

JIM: Don't they take it off the card?

MACY: No the card's not money it's just owing. And if you don't pay right away you gotta pay tax.

JIM: Jeez. Just for using the card?

MACY: That's right.

JIM: It'd be cheaper just to pay right away.

MACY: That's why I ain't got a credit card. It's cheaper.

JIM: When I get disabled they gonna put it right in, help you get the bank and all.

MACY: Just don't let 'em give ya a credit card. You'll be in the poorhouse before ya know.

JIM: I ain't gettin' no credit card. Better ta stand in line.

Pause.

Jeez I'm hungry.

MACY: Get a donut.

JIM: Ain't got enough.

MACY: Get the day olds. They're cheaper.

JIM: How much?

MACY: Don't know. Fifty cents.

JIM: That ain't bad. First good news I heard today. They got all kinds?

MACY: Just what's left.

JIM: Choc'lit?

MACY: Just what's left. That what day olds is.

Pause.

JIM: Maybe I will. *(Pause.)* Gettin' cold.

MACY: Sure is.

JIM: Gotta get a coat.

MACY: Oh yah.

JIM: Ya sleep outside they gives ya a sleepin' bag, but you live inside ya gotta buy yer own coat.

MACY: Coat is a priority.

JIM: I prefer sleeping inside. Gets cold.

MACY: Oh yah. Lot a Indians sleepin' outside.

JIM: They prefer it. Their ancestrals did it.

(Pause.) That's a raw deal eh?

MACY: What?

JIM: Buyin' a coat.

MACY: Yah. Jeez I better get goin'.

JIM: You gotta coat?

MACY: At the club.

JIM: Jeez is it warm there?

MACY: Yah. You got the bath there. It's warm.

JIM: If it gets too cold, ya sleep outside one night, get a sleepin' bag and take it back to the club.

MACY: Yah.

JIM: If ya sewed you could make it into a coat.

MACY: Skills are a necessity.

JIM: Never learned sewing.

MACY: It's easy. Taught myself.

JIM: Ain't that somethin'.

MACY: Education is a necessity. Try an' teach myself somethin' every day.

JIM: I admire them people. I wasn't no good at school.

MACY: Don't need school ta make yourself smart.

JIM: All them subjects. Hist'ry, maths. English. I wasn't good at any. Never cared.

MACY: Math is a necessity.

JIM: What'd math ever do for me?

MACY: Lets you count your change. Lets you buy the right size coat. Tells you how tall you is.

JIM: That's measurin'.

MACY: It's the same thing. It's all math.

JIM: Measurin' is math?

MACY: Measuring and buyin' donuts and changing the channels. It's all the same.

JIM: How's the channels math?

MACY: It's got numbers don't it? Numbers are the center of math. You ain't got math how do you know which go up and which are down?

JIM: Hunh. Channels is math.

MACY: An' history's a necessity. You got no history, then who are you? What'd you do yesterday? You wanna die like your old man with burned up lips?

JIM: No.

MACY: You gotta know yer history. You wanna live the same thing everyday, never have no change?

JIM: No.

MACY: History's important.

JIM: Know your hist'ry.

MACY: An' English is what yer speakin' ta me so you must a learned something at school.

JIM: Yah. *(Beat.)* I always thought I was no good.

MACY: School never did nothin' fer me. I'm goin'.

He stands.

JIM: Oh yah. OK. Me too. *(He stands.)*

MACY: Where ya going?

JIM: Ta vote. One Indian is a lot. That's a fair trade.

MACY: Yah. I guess.

JIM: See ya at the tavern? Specials tonight.

MACY: Oh yah? Maybe.

JIM: OK. Which ways the voting?

MACY: Don't know. See ya. *(MACY goes.)*

JIM: OK. I'll find it. See ya.

JIM stands around confused not knowing what to do. Finally he pulls out a harmonica and begins to play. He puts his hand out for change to passers by.

Blackout.

Scene 2

The same bench. Night time. MACY is sleeping on the bench. JIM enters playing harmonica. A relentless but inspired tune. He is drunk and has a swollen bloody eye. He has no jacket. He plays for awhile then makes his way over to the bench where MACY is curled up. He makes a place to sit and plays another hurrah on the harmonica. He looks around and then at MACY whom he does not recognize.

JIM: That's a fifteen cent song Mr. Hey Mr. Mr. Fifteen cents. Gimme fifteen cents. *(He hits him.)*

MACY: *(Suddenly startled.)* What!

JIM: Gimme fifteen cents. I ain't even got fifteen cents.

MACY: Jeez! Aw jeez ya scared me! What the hell ya think yer doin'. *(He begins to rub his left arm and winces.)* Christ ya made my blood cold.

JIM: Gimme quarter. Just a quarter.

MACY: Scare me half ta death. *(He takes a pill out of his pocket and puts it under his tongue.)*

JIM: Gimme quarter.

MACY: Must'a fell asleep.

JIM: I ain't got nothin'

MACY: Got yer health.

JIM: What good it's done me?

MACY: Keeps ya healthy.

MACY pulls out a full packet of tobacco and rolls a cigarette.

JIM: Gimme smoke Mr.

MACY: Alright. Just don't do that ta fellow sleepin' Jeez what's the matter with ya. What happen to yer eye Jim?

JIM: How'd ya know I'm Jim.

MACY: I metcha before. It's Macy.

JIM: Please ta know ya. You look like a friend a mines. Been to the tavern. Oh yah.

MACY: What happened to yer face?

JIM: Got punched by an epilectric. At the tavern. My girlfriend's boyfriend showed.

MACY: Why'd he hit ya?

JIM: I hit him first.

MACY: What for?

JIM: He took her back. Well she wanted to go. But I hit him.

MACY: Did ya get him?

JIM: Oh yah. Got him good. She can go with him I don't care. I don't care if she goes. She's stupid. She bought me a pitcher though. Yah, I'll miss her but I don't care. First pitcher she ever bought me. She's so cheap. But she's gone. Oh well.

MACY: Here

JIM: Thanks. That's a good smoke. Fresh. Gimme some? I ain't got none.

MACY: I got nothin' ta put it in.

JIM: I'll keep it in my pocket.

MACY gives him some tobacco.

That's good. Ya got papers?

He gives him some.

That's good. Now I got somethin'. Whata ya sleepin' on a bench? *(Pause.)* Yah been drinkin'?

MACY: Before. *(Long pause.)* I saw Rich tonight.

JIM: Who's Rich.

MACY: From the club. Tall fella, silver hair.

JIM: Oh yah. Rich. I know him.

MACY: He died ya know.

JIM: No.

MACY: Strangest thing. I'm at the club. I'm sittin' with Cyril. You know fat Cyril?

JIM: Don't know him.

MACY: Big fat guy? Anyway. We had a coffee. Tellin' me how he used ta had his own business an' all. Pretty wife. An' he owed a loan to the bank an' they took it all away from him. Lost the wife, everythin'.

JIM: Jeez them banks is strict.

MACY: So it's gettin' on. I'm thinkin' I gotta head out 'cause it's gettin' dark, right.

JIM: Yah.

MACY: So's I leave the lounge to take a shower. Wash myself and all, an' there's nobody else around, even the Indians has gone out.

JIM: Yah.

MACY: So I get dressed and I come into the dorm ta get my coat and there's Rich, sittin' on my bed. Big smile. Just sittin'. Scared the life outta me. I'm just standin' there, froze.

JIM: Was he shakin' pennies in his hand?

MACY: Yah. He was. An' he blinks his eyes at me an' they're all sparklin'. He's just starin' at me. Strange look. Finally I get my tongue back an' I says "Jeez, Rich where ya been?" And he don't say nothin'. I ask him if he wants to go to the bar and he just keeps starin'. So I cross over to him and he disappears.

JIM: No.

MACY: Vanished. I thought, you're under a lotta stress. Better get a drink.

JIM: That's creepy. Where'd ya go?

MACY: Up there.

JIM: Oh yah. I thought I saw him too. Las' week. Shakin' a handful a pennies. Rich died eh? Maybe he ain't fully dead.

MACY: What d'ya mean, ain't fully?

JIM: You know floatin', like clouds. Maybe he just wanted to sit an' rest a bit. I could understand. Ghosts must get tired.

MACY: Yah. Shook me. One minute he's there and then gone.

JIM: Yah that was Rich. *(Pause.)* Gettin' cold.

MACY: Where's yer jacket?

JIM: Don't know. Maybe at the tavern still. It's closed.

MACY: You'd better go home. You'll be sick.

JIM: I'm not going back to my sister's. Hey Shorty! I didn't recanize ya. It's Jim.

MACY: I know.

JIM: My sister's stupid, stupid. She don't want me there no more. I wouldn't stay anyway. What she ever done for me? *(Pause.)* Better eat soon. I feel oozy.

MACY: It's all closed now.

JIM: Ain't that donut place open twenty fer hours?

MACY: No. Closes fer two hours.

JIM: Jeez. Not even twenty fer hours in a day no more. Got any food?

MACY: Got a Twizzlers.

JIM: Those red ones?

MACY: Yah.

JIM: Give it to me? Thanks.

MACY: Gets stuck in my teeth.

JIM: Yah. It's gonna be cold real soon. I don't care.

MACY: How's yer eye?

JIM: It's dried. Don't hurt. I punched him good.

MACY: You're free now.

JIM: Oh yah. No long term. Just get on with it.

MACY: Yah. Did ya vote?

JIM: Vote? Oh no. Who won?

MACY: I don't know.

JIM: Jeez. Hope the Indian won.

MACY: Maybe. Anything can happen.

Pause.

JIM: I don't feel so good.

MACY: Whatsa matter?

JIM: Just sick.

MACY: It'll pass. *(Pause.)*

MACY: Clear sky tonight.

JIM: There's stars.

MACY: Ya.

JIM: I wonder what stars is.

MACY: Don't know.

JIM: Maybe it's where ghosts go when they're finished floatin'.

MACY: Hunh.

JIM: Maybe Rich is gonna be a star soon.

MACY: Maybe. I don't know what they is. *(Pause.)*

JIM: They got extra cots where yer stayin'?

MACY: I ain't stayin' there no more, first thing tomorrow I'm gettin' my stuff. I ain't sleepin' there no more.

JIM: Why not?

MACY: On account 'a the ghost.

JIM: I don't think ghosts'd hurt ya. If I was a ghost I wouldn't hurt nobody. Unless I was mad.

MACY: I ain't stayin' there. Too shook up.

JIM: How's my eye?

MACY: Looks fine to me.

Pause. Jim pulls out his harmonica.

JIM: Wanna hear me play?

MACY: Nah.

JIM: OK. *(Pause.)* Wish I had my jacket. Maybe we stay out here they'll give us sleepin' bags.

MACY: That's only in winter.

JIM: It's cold now.

MACY: It's only in the winter.

JIM: That a gyp.

MACY: Go to the light house.

JIM: I ain't goin there. It's strict there.

MACY: Yah, but it's cold.

JIM: I'll get a coffee later. *(Pause.)* She can go with him. Never did nothin' fer me. *(Pause.)* I'll miss her though.

MACY: She pretty?

JIM: Yah. Real pretty. He'll prob'ly have a fit, then she'll come back. I ain't concerned. *(He almost slips to the ground.)*

MACY: Jeez, careful. Almost fell off the bench.

JIM: Feel a bit oozy. Got a smoke?

MACY: Gave ya some.

JIM: No.

MACY: In yer pocket.

JIM: Oh yah. I got some.

MACY: What's the matter at yer sister's?

JIM: She got more stupid. Her husband don't want me there no more.

MACY: How come.

JIM: He says I owe her money fer stayin'. Couldn't ever even bring Marge over.

MACY: Jeez. That's family fer ya.

JIM: My own sister. What I ever done to her? Nothin'. When I die an' get ta be a ghost, I'm goin' back to haunt her. Or my brother in law's bus. Let every one on for free. Then I'll keep floatin' up to the stars an jus' sparkle forever.

He falls off the bench onto the ground.

MACY: Jeez you OK?

JIM: I feel oozy.

MACY: Let me help ya. Come on, lift yerself up. Can't ya get up? Jim. Jim you OK?

JIM: Oh yah, I's jus' lookin' at the stars. They sure is nice.

MACY: Yah. Let's get ya up. The groun's too cold.

JIM: I'm gonna sleep here for awhile.

MACY: It's too cold.

JIM: Nah, it's OK. Yah got any family Shorty?

MACY: No. Jus' me.

JIM: Me too. I ain't got no one.

MACY: Ya got yerself.

JIM: Na. What good's that done me?

MACY: Gets ya up everyday. Let's ya enjoy a smoke.

JIM: Ya wanna smoke? I got some.

MACY: Na. Ya gotta have a piece of yerself or you'd just die.

JIM: You gotta piece 'a yerself?

MACY: Somewheres.

Pause.

JIM: Got any money?

MACY: Yah.

JIM: That's good too.

Pause.

Sleepy. Hey Shorty.

MACY: Yah.

JIM: C'mere a minute.

MACY: What for?

JIM: C'mere.

He does.

MACY: Yah.

JIM: You want my harmonica?

MACY: Why'd ya wanna give away yer harmonica?

JIM: I ain't so good on it. Maybe you'll be good on it.

MACY: Never had no musical talent.

JIM: Don't matter. Ya play an' people'll give ya money. Lots 'a pennies but sometimes a quarter.

MACY: Na. You keep it. Ya might need it sometime.

JIM: Na. I'm retired. I'll get another job. Maybe whistlin'. I'll show ya. Not now 'cause I just retired. I'll show ya soon

MACY: OK Jim.

JIM: I'll show ya soon.

MACY: OK Jimmy.

JIM falls asleep. MACY sits there beside him for awhile. He then takes the harmonica and plays a soft sweet note. He puts the harmonica back.

I used ta play good. *(He suddenly gets a strong shiver. He turns and looks behind him.)* Gettin' cold.

JIM snorts in his sleep. MACY looks over at him. He takes his coat off and throws it over their two bodies and lies down beside him. As lights slowly fade JIM rolls on his side pulling the coat off of MACY. Leaves blow in the wind. TOM enters drunk. He stands at a distance and looks at the sleeping men. Then he crosses, lays down on the bench and goes to sleep.

Black out.

Act II

The bench. Three months later. Winter. The stage is littered with snow. SHORTY wanders on in a daze, in his socks, T-shirt and pants. One of his hands is clenched shut. Some of his clothes are burnt. His hands and face are somewhat blackened. A fire truck beacon flashes offstage. SHORTY approaches the bench but collapses before reaching it. He sits on the ground. Folds his arms to keep himself warm. He looks around, confused, then stares straight ahead. TOM enters with a sleeping bag around him. He shuffles along until he sees SHORTY and approaches him. He looks around, then speaks.

TOM: Cold.

(Pause.) S'only gonna get worse. *(Pause.)* 'Fore gets better. *(Pause.)* That's fer sure.

Pause.

Should sit on a bench. S'warmer.

Pause.

(Sniffing the air.) Smells smokey. Someone's dryin' fish. Hunh. *(Pause.)* You like fish? *(Silence.)* Had an uncle, smoked his own. Caught 'em summer, ate 'em all winter. *(Pause.)* Goldeye, pickerel, catfish. Master smoker. Died 'a cancer. Maybe he smoked his self. *(Pause.)* Now all they got is them fish sticks. Powdered fish. Used ta catch cod five feet tall. Now it's all mercury, cancer. See em, dead

fishes on the shore. Mouths gapin' not knowin' what was happenin'. *(Pause.)* Drowned in dried up lakes. *(Beat.)* Smells like fire. Hunh. *(Pause.)* All matchsticks 'round here. Goin' up alla time. *(Pause.)* Them roomin' houses. Fire traps. Go in, fire starts, you're trapped. *(Squinting.)* Mus' be a fire truck there or maybe ambulance. *(Realizing.)* Ya there's a fire there I'm pretty sure. *(Pause.)* That's no good. Safer ta live in a street. Shorty shivers Cold eh? *(Pause.)* Want my sleepin' bag? *(Pause.)* S'OK. I'll find another one. *(He puts it around SHORTY.)* Cold is a state 'a mind. *(Pause.)* Got any booze? *(No response.)* Booze is like a sleepin' bag. Keeps ya zipped up. Ha ha. *(Pause.)* I used to had a real buffalo coat. When I was a kid eh, that was warm. *(Pause.)* Soft buffalo hide. My grandfather got it at a flea market. *(Pause.)* That was the best coat I had. *(Sits beside him.)* Not many buffalo now. I never seen one. *(Pause.)* Hunh. Buffalo hide. *(Pause.)* Ya can't see em. Buffalo hide. Ha ha. *(Pause.)* Got any booze?

MACY: Walla. Beat Walla.

TOM: What?

MACY: Walla.

TOM: What's walla?

MACY: *(Beginning hysterically and growing calm.)* Walla…walla…walla fire. Out…side the door. Walla fire…was hot. Hot! Hot! Hot and I could, couldn't, couldn't… I ran in, into the fla…fla… flames 'cause, it was cccomin' into the room and it ate ate ate up the carpet and and I couldn't, couldn't…sssee my way…on ma ma my knees 'cause the smo smoke wa was thick and Morgan and Cccyril and and and Lana they…Lana she was… She didn't… Lana…we went for… for drinks on? So pretty. Kiss…kissed… Then the stairs fell away she got....under, trapped under,...and I, I tried to get get her but the ceiling caved...an she was under the ceiling and the sssstairway and she grabbed my my my hand but...the trucks came but couldn't... *(Pause. Calmer.)* ...and then the wall came down, just dropped and I was outside and I walked away. 'Cause I wanted to sit.

Pause.

TOM: You was in the fire?

MACY: Ya.

TOM: Up there?

MACY: Ya.

TOM: Holy smokes. You get burned?

MACY: Don't know.

TOM: Does it hurt?

MACY: Don't know.

TOM: You prob'ly got shocked.

(He stares off.) Looks bad. *(Beat.)* Gonna be a lot less sleepin' bags soon. They ain't gonna have enough. *(Warning him.)* Could 'a got smoked in there. *(Pause.)* People ain't no different than charcoal once they're burnin'. *(Pause.)* Money an' clothes ain't nothin, but yer hands and skin, you need those. Yer hair. *(Pause.)* Had a fire on the reserve when I was a little guy. My sister, my aunt got smoked. Bad. There faces frozen, fightin' for breath. *(Pause.)* Fire's a bad way to go.

MACY: Walla flame.

TOM: Oh ya.

MACY: *(Distracted.)* Everything...alive. The floor... dresser. Lana on fire.

TOM: Yer old lady?

MACY: All burnin'. It weren't her no more.

TOM: That's tough. Losin' your ol' lady is tough. *(Beat.)* I seen lots 'a fires 'round here. Everyone loses somethin'. Friends is the worst.

(Beat.) It's changin'. That's fer sure. *(Pause.)* They're burnin' us out. Real estate's worth a million dollars to 'em. They don't care. One old lady ain't nothin' to a million dollars.

MACY: She...she was... La...la, la, Laaaanaaa! *(He breaks down.)*

TOM: You should talk to someone. You're shocked. Talkin's good when you had a shock. I had plenty shocks and talkin' takes the shocks away. Once you done that you see clear.

MACY: I see clear.

TOM: No, it's too early.

MACY: *(He grows suddenly intense.)* It's all burnin'. You're on fire, the bench, the sky, the ground. Everythin' burnin'.

Beat.

TOM: That's good, talking's good.

MACY: Flamin' people running around! They been burnin' a long time. They just finally exploded.

TOM: Why didn't you burn up?

MACY: Didn't get hot enough yet.

TOM: Hunh.

MACY: I ain't hot enough.

Pause.

TOM: Yer hand burned?

MACY opens his hand, there is a ring inside.

It's a ring.

MACY: Where'd I get…? Maybe it's Lana's. Maybe it come from her burning hand.

TOM: Prob'ly want ya ta have it.

SHORTY grabs his left arm and suffers a short angina attack. Pause.

You OK Mr?

MACY: Hey.

TOM: What?

MACY: My…my pills.

TOM: What?

MACY: My pills. Check my pockets.

TOM: *(He checks.)* Nothin'.

MACY: Inside.

TOM: *(He checks.)* A kleenex.

MACY: *(The attack subsides.)* My pills, my coat. My pictures. All burned.

TOM: Pills ain't no good. They mix ya up. Had me on pills. They get ya on pills so ya don't go around remembrin' who you are.

MACY: It's all burnin'. Your eyes are on fire.

TOM: What?

MACY: There's flames in yer mouth.

TOM: Hunh.

Pause.

What're you gonna do?

MACY: Wait 'till I get hot enough.

TOM: Ya. Nothing going on.

(Pause.) Got any booze?

Silence.

TOM: Stayin' out ain't bad. *(Pause.)* Go on the wrong corner, you find trouble. I stay outta trouble. *(Pause.)* Growin' up taught me somethin'. *(Pause.)* Ya, I don't know.

MACY: *(Lookin' at him.)* You Indian?

TOM: Anishnawbe. *First Nations.*

MACY: First what?

TOM: Nations.

MACY: What d'ya want?

TOM: Nothin'.

MACY: I ain't got no money.

TOM: Didn't ask for none.

MACY: Ain't got none. Lost everythin'.

TOM: *(Pause.)* That's tough.

MACY: Ya ain't gettin' my ring.

TOM: Don't want it.

MACY: You better move on.

TOM: Nothin' goin' on, it's early.

MACY: It's illegal to sit in groups. Cops'll come.

TOM: I got nowhere to go. *(Pause.)* Hardly no place to sleep. All patrolled now, *(Pause.)* Hunh. *(Beat.)* At school back home, church school you know, used ta tell us—be whatever you want, doctor, astronaut. Believe, an' Jesus would answer yer dreams. I wanted to be a pilot. You know, fly airplanes. *(Pause.)* Could happen. *(Pause.)* Ya. I don't know.

MACY: Indians got it easy.

TOM: We ain't got nothin' easy.

MACY: Millions from the gover'ment fer housin' and fishin'.

TOM: Them houses ain't no good.

MACY: All that money to schools and programs.

TOM: Them schools is bein' examined. Aw that was somethin'. Them priests wasn't there for Jesus, they was there for Indians. That's fer sure. *(Pause.)* Now they wanna get us money from suin' the church but no one wants to talk about that. Better to burn it down.

MACY: *(Looking at the ring.)* Lana. Poor Lana.

Pause.

TOM: Them priests put somethin' in our food eh? Try an' make us dumb. Only comin' here is when I learned anythin'. At that centre.

MACY: What centre?

TOM: Downtown. By the welfare.

MACY: Waste a money.

TOM: No. They got a libary. All the old stories. No Jesus in any of it.

MACY: Leave Jesus alone.

TOM: I like Jesus but he wasn't no Indian. My people been here a long time without Jesus. Them missionaries brought him. We was livin' with nature. Fishing, planting.

(Pause.) You like corn. Hey, you like corn?

MACY: Ya.

TOM: Indians changed the world with corn.

MACY: What?

TOM: Corn cakes, corn bread. Corn changed the economy. Indians gave corn to the world.

MACY: Popcorn?

TOM: That's Indian. All corn is Indian.

MACY: Them Corn Puffs?

TOM: Indian.

MACY: Lana liked them Corn Puffs.

Pause.

TOM: All Indian. My people didn't need nothin from the white man. They had corn. Have a corn patch, live off the earth. Feed the earth, earth feeds you. My people always known that. Look at the sun and moon. It's all circles. Can't get nothin if you don't give back. My grandad taught me that. Healing man, like Jesus. Died abetes. Wouldn't take his insular.

(Pause.) If I could, I'd go backwards. Sit by a corn patch smokin' with my grandad. Hunh. *(Beat.)* D'I ask if ya had any booze?

Long pause. JIM enters on a motor cart, dressed for winter in a poverty chic with sunglasses, a scarf and a case of beer in the wagon. He stops gets off the cart and looks at the fire.

JIM: What's goin' on?

TOM: Fire.

JIM: Where?

TOM: Up there.

JIM: What burned?

TOM: Don't know.

JIM: Smells like meat. There's a butcher up there, Mel's. Porkchops thick as yer fist.

(Concerned.) Jeez. Be a shame if he lost the shop. Butchers is a dyin' art.

TOM: Guy got smoked in the fire.

JIM: He get burned?

TOM: He don't know.

JIM: *(To MACY.)* You got injuries?

TOM: He don't know.

MACY: I don't know.

TOM: That ain't good. *(Pause.)* He could be shocked.

JIM: Ya.

TOM: Yer s'posed to keep 'em warm.

JIM: Good thing he had a sleepin' bag. Well see ya. *(He starts to climb back on to the cart.)*

TOM: Got any booze?

JIM: What?

TOM: Anything to drink? Booze?

Beat.

JIM: Ya.

TOM: Give me a drink.

JIM: A drink?

TOM: Ya. You got bourbon?

JIM: No.

TOM: Rye?

JIM: No.

TOM: I like wine.

JIM: No sorry, all's I got is beer. *(He gets on the cart.)*

TOM: I like beer.

JIM: You didn't mention beer.

TOM: I mentioned beer.

JIM: I don't think…

TOM: I like it. I mentioned it. I did.

JIM: *(Beat.)* OK, it's only that sometimes I can't remember so I thought you didn't mention it.

(He gets off the cart.) OK. You can have a beer but then I gotta go. *(He gives him one.)*

TOM: You can go.

JIM: I need the bottle.

TOM: Hunh?.

JIM: I need the refund on the bottle, that way next time I buy beer I ain't gotta pay for the bottle, just the beer. The bottle comes free.

(l to r): Ron Gabriel (Jim), Earl Pastko (Shorty) and Lorne Cardinal (Big Tom)

TOM: Hunh.

JIM: So hurry up so I can go.

TOM: Have one too. Better than drinking alone.

JIM: Ya got the TV. Ya ain't alone.

TOM: I ain't got no TV.

JIM: Then you don't know what yer missing. Which is good I guess. Anyway, Hurry up I gotta go.

(Beat. He adjusts his scarf.) I been looking into getting cable, but I ain't convinced. It's expensive. But sometimes they play it for free anyways, on a weekend.

TOM: Hunh. I don't know.

JIM: Oh jeez ya, I'm tellin' ya, we don't know what we're missin'. *(Beat.)* Howza beer?

TOM: Cold.

JIM: Ya. Beer's colder in winter.

(Beat.) Maybe I will join ya. I got enough. *(He gets one. He looks at the bottle.)* This beer has no name. It's cheaper cause it ain't got a name. I'm Jim.

TOM: Thanks for the beer.

JIM: Jeez don't mention it, it ain't even got a name.

Beat.

TOM: Fire's still goin'.

JIM: Must be one of them five o'clock fires. What time is it?

TOM: Don't know.

JIM: Oh wait I got it. *(He looks at his watch.)* No, almost seven. Looks pretty bad.

TOM: Ya.

JIM: You in the fire too?

TOM: No jus' him.

JIM: In a roomin' house?

TOM: Don't know. Was it in a roomin' house? Hey, was it a roomin' house!?

MACY: Ya.

TOM: I think so.

JIM: Jeez. Got insurance? *(Beat.)* Ask him if he got insurance.

TOM: Ya insured?

MACY: What?

TOM: Ya got insurance!

MACY: No.

TOM: No.

JIM: Ya got insurance they take care of ya in a fire. I'm gonna get some but I'm thinking about cable. I'm planning it out slowly.

TOM: You win the bingo?

JIM: Disabled benefit. You could prob'ly get it. Twice the welfare.

TOM: Need an address?

JIM: I used my sister.

TOM: Where she live?

JIM: Up there. But you'd have to ask, she's pretty stuck up.

TOM: Ya I don't know.

JIM: You could get disabled no problem.

(Whispering.) It's the rooming house people they gotta watch out for. They scam the government. That's why the gover'ment's broke. Scamming. They don't care, they're scammers.

TOM: Hunh.

JIM: They set up phones. You can put em in jail so they don't steal your taxes no more. Now I ain't sayin', cause I know there's lots a Indians in jail, I ain't sayin' Indians is scammers, alls I'm sayin' is Indians should be announced disabled and get some money before it's all gone. Ask that fella.

TOM: Which fella?

JIM: You got that Indian now.

TOM: Who?

JIM: Ain't there an Indian in the goverment?

TOM: Nobody's gonna elect no Indian in the gover'ment.

JIM: *(Beat.)* Well you should talk to someone.

TOM: *(To MACY.)* Hey! Want some beer?

Silence.

MACY: Ya.

TOM: He wants a beer and I ain't got none.

JIM: Ya.

TOM: *(Pause.)* He wants one, the guy who got smoked.

MACY: Macy.

TOM: You got two beers there?

JIM: *(Suspicious.)* If I give you one, and him is two. And you had one is three.

TOM: *(Pause.)* Ya.

JIM: And how many did he have?

TOM: He didn't have none. You had one.

JIM: Right, that's four. And if I give him and you is six. I only got twelve. I won't have none left.

TOM: You got more.

JIM: Ya but they're going fast. I just got it and it's almost gone.

TOM: You got more.

JIM: Then I should get one too. I only had one. If you get two I should get one too.

TOM: That's fair.

JIM: So then how many do I have left?

Pause.

MACY: What ever's in the case.

JIM: Right. OK. *(He gets the beers.)* As long as what's left is mines. Drink em fast, I need the bottles. *(Beat.)* Fire's pretty big. You could clean up if ya had insurance eh?

TOM: I dunno.

JIM: Oh ya. You could clean up.

Silence.

MACY: I used ta live there.

JIM: Where?

MACY: Greyson's.

JIM: The roomin' house?

MACY: Ya.

JIM: *(Distraught.)* Is Greyson's the place on fire?

MACY: Ya.

JIM: Then the butcher's is gone for sure. Poor Mel. You ever shop there?

MACY: Ya.

JIM: All that meat. It's all cooked.

MACY: Help me up.

TOM: You gonna get up?

MACY: To the bench.

TOM: OK. Easy steady.

SHORTY stands.

JIM: Hey Shorty! It's me Jim. I never recanized you.

MACY: Who?

JIM: Jim. Jim. I seen ya before.

MACY: I don't know.

JIM: What d'ya mean. It's Jim.

TOM: He's still shocked. He thinks everyone's on fire. Hey, is he on fire too?

MACY: Ya.

TOM: He's shocked.

JIM: He knows me. I'm just changed is all.

TOM: What's changed?

JIM: I'm in a program. Shorty. They put me in a

program for the disableds. I didn't wanna go but they wouldn't a given me a check. So there's twelve of us. They're doin' a study of us twelve disables. They give ya a place to live and money and someone helps you organize the money and change yerself. You got a meetin' every month and you keep a record of the changes.

TOM: What for?

JIM: To see if you're changed.

MACY: *(Referring to the beer.)* Can you open this.

TOM: Sure.

JIM: See most people on benefits don't do nothing to fix themselves. So it's a test to see if it's possible to fix us.

TOM: Sounds hard.

JIM: It ain't hard. See the problem is most people is lazy right? They'd rather scam the goverment than fix themselves. So you follow, I think it's twelve steps, to save money and fix yourself. Listen Shorty, once you save, I think it's two hundred dollars, they invest it for you, so you gotta live on a budget to get the inves'ment.

Once it's worth I think it's a thousand dollars they put it some place else for you and all you gotta do is wait.

And then when it's worth…well it keeps going up 'cause it's all mutual right and when the gover'ment thinks it's time, they ask the bank and the bank sends you a check. It's all central now, it's all connected. Pretty sweet hunh?

(Beat.) So Shorty, how ya been ? I ain't seen ya in awhile.

MACY: Getting hot.

TOM: You got any money?

JIM: No.

MACY: Your face is smoking.

JIM: What?

TOM: You got money. You just said.

JIM: That was a private discussion, you shouldn't a been listenin' to that. That money's invested for retirin'.

TOM: You got change?

JIM: No.

TOM: From the beer.

JIM: Didn't use money. Used a card. So Shorty…

TOM: What card?

JIM: Bank card. Take it right outta your account. Jus' pin your card and it's paid. *(Turns to SHORTY.)*

TOM: How'd you get it?

JIM: It's part 'a the program. Jeez. See the banks don't want us carryin' money no more, 'cause it's too expensive. So now you use a card, it's cheaper for the banks.

TOM: Is it free?

JIM: Ya they give 'em free. You gotta pay when you use it but it's cheap.

TOM: How much?

JIM: About a dollar. It's cheap. In the old days I used ta never have no money, now you don't need none.

TOM: I'm gonna get one.

JIM: Everyone's got 'em. Shorty, you got a bank card?

Silence.

MACY: Cold.

JIM: You cold?

MACY: The beer. Cold.

JIM: Ya.

Pause.

TOM: Where'd ya get the car?

JIM: It ain't a car, it's a Sun Rider. From the gover'ment. If I gotta go talk to the bank or see the gover'ment I gotta be mobile. It's part of the program. Sun Rider. Came with the basket.

TOM: How fast does it go?

JIM: Pretty fast.

TOM: Hunh.

JIM: You can look but don't sit on it.

TOM crosses to the cart. JIM sits beside SHORTY and slaps his knee.

Hey Shorty, how ya been?

Pause.

SHORTY: Not bad.

TOM: *(He sits on the cart.)* He lost his old lady.

JIM: *(Shocked.)* No.

TOM: Ya, in the fire.

JIM: Did they find her?

TOM: She got burned up.

MACY: My pants is on fire.

JIM: She burned up? At the rooming house?

TOM: I think so.

JIM: Who's your old lady?

TOM beeps the horn.

Don't do that!

TOM: It's pretty loud eh. How fast does it go?

JIM: Hey Shorty, who died in the fire?

MACY: Lana, Cyril…Morgan.

JIM: Morgan? The black guy with the tooth?

MACY: Yah.

JIM: He died?

MACY: Yah.

TOM: It's got a light too.

JIM: Turn it off. Morgan. Jeez. He was a funny guy. And when he laughed he looked funny too. Morgan burned up eh? Jeez. And who else?

MACY: Lana and Cyril.

JIM: Cyril? Don't know him.

MACY: Good friend a mine.

JIM: That's tough, losin' a friend is tough. You think you'll always have em, then they're gone. *(Pause.)* Who's Lara?

MACY: Lana.

JIM: Lana? Who's she? Oh wait, she a skinny red head? Dimple on her forehead?

MACY: Ya.

JIM: She died?

MACY: Feels hot in my chest.

TOM: *(Crossing to the bench.)* That's a nice car.

JIM: Lana was in the program. She was a test woman in the program. She was your old lady? She never mentioned that. *(Growing increasingly worried.)* This is going to be bad for the program. They ain't gonna be able to assess the results if we only got eleven. This could be a big change…for the study…if it fails… *(He pulls out a writing book and pen from his pocket.)* Lana…What was Lana's last name?

MACY: Don't know.

JIM: Writing "Lana…blank died in a fire".

TOM: What are ya doing?

JIM: Gotta keep a record a things that happen. Then we discuss what we could a done to change it. *(He starts to write, then thinks.)* But I couldn't a changed it, I wasn't there. *(Beat.)* …I better make a note about that.

He starts to write.

TOM: You get that car free?

JIM: Sh! I'm making notes. Did Lana burn up or did she die a smoke?

TOM: You shouldn't ask that, he's still getting over it.

JIM: Hey Shorty, smoked or burned?

MACY: Burned.

JIM: *(Writing.)* Aw jeez. I don't know which is worse.

TOM: *(Crosses to Macy.)* What're you gonna do now?

MACY: Wait to explode.

TOM: This ain't a good corner, guy got knifed las' month. You don't wanna wait here.

JIM: You at Greyson's too?

TOM: No.

JIM: Where you stayin'?

TOM: Up there.

JIM: Oh ya. They got space for him?

TOM: *(To MACY.)* You wanna sit around with a buncha First Nations?

MACY: Beer's gettin' warm.

JIM: What's a First Nations?

TOM: My people is First Nations.

JIM: I thought you was Indians.

TOM: No.

JIM: When'd it change?

TOM: Always been First Nations, Indians is a made up name.

JIM: Who made it up?

TOM: I don't know.

JIM: *(Writing.)* "Indians is now First Nations. Things is changin' fast." *(He puts his book away.)* That empty?

TOM: Ya. *(TOM gives JIM his empty bottle.)*

JIM: Hey you finished with that bottle? Shorty, you finished?

MACY: No.

JIM: Well hurry up, I gotta go. *(Beat. Slaps his back.)* So how ya been Shorty? *(Beat.)* I gotta have you up to my place.

TOM: You gotta place?

JIM: *(To SHORTY.)* You should come up. I got porkchops inna freezer. Big as your hand. What's the matter with your hand?

MACY: *(Opens his hand. Surprised.)* Ring.

JIM: Where'd you get it?

Beat.

MACY: It was Lana's.

JIM: Is it real?

MACY: Don't know.

JIM: Was it a present?

MACY: Came off her hand in the fire.

JIM: Can I see? Let me see.

SHORTY: Careful. It's still hot.

He hands him the ring. JIM looks at the inside.

JIM: Pretty nice. Somethin' scratched in the back.

(Reading.) Lara Burns. That her name Lara Burns?

MACY: Lana.

JIM: That's it, Lana Burns! She's the one from the group. Oh boy this is big! This is evidence Shorty!

MACY: What?

JIM: They're gonna need this to identify. To bury her. The gover'ment has gotta have this ring.

MACY: It's my ring.

JIM: It come off in the fire Shorty. That's what ya said.

TOM: It's his ring.

JIM: Gover'ment's gotta have this. They won't recanize her without it.

SHORTY: Recanize what, she's dead.

JIM: They gotta ratify her. This has gotta be handed in.

MACY: Give it back.

TOM: Give it to him.

JIM: Shorty. I'd let ya keep it but… You come with me. You tell the police you found it.

MACY: I ain't goin' nowhere.

TOM: Want me to hit him?

JIM: It ain't a long walk. I'll drive slow.

MACY: I ain't movin'.

TOM: Should I hit him?

JIM: Shorty, if you was burned and no one recanized ya, they wouldn't have a name for your stone. How'd you feel if no one came to visit you?

MACY: I couldn't care less!

JIM: The gover'ment's gotta give this to her family.

TOM: *(Grabbing JIM.)* Why'd ya take his ring?

JIM: It ain't me, it's the gover'ment.

TOM: Give him his ring or I'm gonna knock you.

JIM: If she ain't got no family he can have it back, otherwise it's to put up a stone.

TOM: I'm gonna count to three.

MACY: Give me Lana's ring.

JIM: It's Lara Shorty. Even you don't recanize her no more.

MACY: It's Lana!

TOM: Want me to hit him? I'm gonna count to three.

JIM: Don't count to three. Shorty, as part of the program I gotta report auspicious things. And you havin' Lana's ring is an auspicious thing.

MACY: I didn't start the fire.

JIM: No one is sayin' ya did. I didn't say that. A judge may not see it as auspicious. Unless you don't turn it in.

TOM: *(To MACY.)* You want me to count?

JIM: Don't count.

MACY: *(Angry.)* Give me my ring!

TOM: *(To MACY.)* You want me to?

MACY: *(Pleading.)* It's all I got! I ain't got nothing!

Pause.

JIM: It's the only thing left 'a her Shorty. *(Beat.)* You wanna take the only thing left? It's all that's left. *(Beat.)* Let her rest in peace.

Pause.

TOM: Should I count?

MACY: *(Beaten.)* Let him go. *(Pause.)*

JIM: Now my clothes is rumpled.

MACY: I jus' wanted somethin' to remember.

JIM: Remembrin' ain't no good. I don't remember nothin' an' look at me. You should worry about the future. That's comin' sooner.

TOM: *(To MACY.)* You givin' him the ring?

JIM: That's between me and him. *(To MACY.)* You done the right thing Shorty. I'll turn it in and tell em yer name as the one who found it. Maybe they'll give it to ya when her stone is up. But don't worry about that, you gotta look after yourself now. *(He puts the ring in his pocket and talks low.)* It's been a long time I ain't seen ya but I'm surprised, Look at ya. Shorty, ya gotta look after yourself, make sure, down the road, if the time comes, you got a future.

Now me? I'm slowly making plans all the time. That's the secret. You and me is the same except I'm slowly making plans all the time.

I'm thinkin' what money can do for me instead of the other way around, see? This group I'm in, you should try an' get in, it's twelve of…no now it's eleven but what they teach is how to be tools of financial success in your later years.

Beat.

I'll tell you what. Since we're old friends, I'll see what I can do about recommendin' you. I can't promise nothin' but there might be a spot opening up. I'll talk to the gover'ment. See what I can do.

Beat.

Shorty I know you're upset 'cause 'a Morgan an' them, but ya gotta plan your next step. That's the secret. Plannin'. Thinkin' 'bout today's a waste a time. Plan the next five, six years now and get a jump on the future. It could come at any time.

Beat.

You want a hug? Let me give ya a hug.

(He hugs him.) OK. That's jus' to show ya I'm here for ya'. It don't mean nothin' else.

(He stands.) I need that bottle now I gotta go. *(He takes the bottle and drains it.)* Think about what I said.

SHORTY suddenly suffers another angina attack. Silence.

JIM: Shorty you OK? *(Beat.)* You got no shoes on! You could freeze your feet off. Look, here, take my gloves. Here I'll put em on your feet for ya. This'll help, they're warm. Is that better? Now they ain't exposed. I'll get em from you later.

TOM: Maybe he needs a doctor.

JIM: *(He speaks low.)* Everyone's running to doctors for nothin'. That's why they took all the money outta hospitals, 'cause people was going and they ain't even sick.

TOM: He looks sick. He should be inside.

JIM: I'd take him but he won't fit on the Sun Rider. He's OK, he's just messed up. You take care of him.

Pause.

You look after him OK?

TOM: OK boss.

JIM: You know, I always had respect for Indians. They ain't scammers, they just got a bad deal because they didn't plan ahead. But you can change that. What's your name?

TOM: Tom.

JIM: Tom. It ain't what happened before that matters,

it's what you do tomorrow that's the matter. You can change yourself. If you try.

TOM: OK boss.

JIM: And don't go counting to three. You'll end up in jail too. *(Staring at the fire.)* Jeez. Used to have pork chop Tuesdays. Poor Mel. It's all gonna be different now.

(He crosses to his Sun Rider.) I'm counting on you. I want a full report. OK. Two, four, six, eight, ten, eleven, twelve. I got all my bottles. See ya.

He drives off. Long pause.

TOM: That guy…

Pause.

MACY: Ya.

Pause.

TOM: How ya feelin'?

MACY: I don't know.

TOM: *(Pause.)* Wanna go to the hospital?

MACY: Na.

Pause.

TOM: Wanna go to the subway?

MACY: Na.

TOM: What do ya wanna do?

MACY: Just sit.

TOM: OK. *(Pause.)* Everythin' still burnin?

MACY: Ya. I'm pretty hot now.

Pause.

TOM: What was I tellin' ya? *(Long pause.)* Oh ya 'bout that corn patch. That'd be good. Me an' my grandad sitting together, smokin'. Watchin' the corn. Corn changed the world. Imagine that. *(Beat.)* You believe in God?

MACY: Na.

TOM: Me neither. *(Beat.)* Too bad. *(Pause.)* You don't got no booze eh?

MACY: No.

TOM: Yah. *(Beat.)* What time is it?

MACY: Don't know.

TOM: I'm s'posed to meet some friends. *(Pause.)* I better get going.

MACY: OK.

TOM: You look after yourself.

MACY: OK.

Pause.

TOM: What's your name?

MACY: Shorty.

TOM: OK, Shorty you look after yourself.

He leaves.

MACY: OK. *(MACY looks at his empty hand.)*

Black out.

The End.